DAILY
PUSH
JOURNAL

THE ULTIMATE PUBLISHING HOUSE (UPH) HEADQUARTERS
Canadian Office: 205 Glen Shields Avenue, Toronto, Ontario, Canada L4K 1T3
Telephone: 647-883-1758
www.ultimatepublishinghouse.com E-mail: info@ultimatepublishinghouse.com
www.PushThroughBook.com
www.ultimatepublishinghouse.com
E-mail: info@ultimatepublishinghouse.com

US OFFICE: Ordering Information
Quantity Sales: Companies, organizations, institutions and industry publications. Quantity discounts are available on bulk purchases of this book for reselling, educational purposes, subscription incentives, gifts, sponsorship, or fundraising. Unique books or book excerpts can also be fashioned to suit special needs such as private labeling with your logo on the cover and a message from or a message printed on the second page of the book. For more information, please contact our
Special Sales Department at Ultimate Publishing House. Orders for college textbook or course adoption use.

Please contact Ultimate Publishing House Tel: 647-883-1758
DAILY PUSH JOURNAL by HAWLEY WOODS & CAREY YUKICH

ISBN: 978-1-7354831-1-5

DAILY PUSH JOURNAL

Date: / /

Many of life's failures are people who did not realize how close they were to success when they gave up. —Thomas Edison

I am grateful for:

1.
2.
3.

My commitments today:

1.
2.

My daily push mindset:

1.

Date: __/__/_____

It's Not Whether You Get Knocked Down,
It's Whether You Get Up. —By Vince Lombardi

I am grateful for:

1. _____
2. _____
3. _____

My commitments today:

1. _____
2. _____

My daily push mindset:

1. _____

_____

_____

_____

_____

_____

_____

Date: ___/___/_____

If You Are Working On Something That You Really Care About, You Don't Have To Be Pushed. The Vision Pulls You.

— Steve Jobs

I am grateful for:

1. _____
2. _____
3. _____

My commitments today:

1. _____
2. _____

My daily push mindset:

1. _____

_____

_____

_____

_____

_____

_____

Date: ___/___/___

People Who Are Crazy Enough To Think They Can Change The World, Are The Ones Who Do. – Rob Siltanen

I am grateful for:

1. _____
2. _____
3. _____

My commitments today:

1. _____
2. _____

My daily push mindset:

1. _____

_____

_____

_____

_____

_____

_____

Date: / /

*Failure Will Never Overtake Me If My Determination
To Succeed Is Strong Enough.* – Og Mandino

I am grateful for:

1.
2.
3.

My commitments today:

1.
2.

My daily push mindset:

1.

Date: ___/___/_____

We May Encounter Many Defeats But We Must Not Be Defeated. – Maya Angelou

I am grateful for:

1. _____
2. _____
3. _____

My commitments today:

1. _____
2. _____

My daily push mindset:

1. _____

_____

_____

_____

_____

_____

_____

_____

Weekly Reflection for My Daily Push Journal

We also want you to commit to 100% participation in this reflection once a week.

The guidelines to give you the best success are:

1. Find a quiet place that is technology- and people-free (aside from music that may lend to focus)

2. Do not rush, stay present, enjoy the journey

3. Find takeaways from each area of evaluation (what you learned, what you need to improve on, what is working, etc.)

Everyone has a way to give this amount of time to their success every week.

Topic to reflect on:

1. *Practice, Practice, Practice*

   a. What areas in the last week have you shown discipline, outlined a routine, or demonstrated strong time management?

   b. What areas in the last week need improvement or more practice in the week ahead?

2. *Just Keep Going*

    a. In the last week, how have you demonstrated perseverance or resilience?

    b. What can you do in the week ahead to improve and/or help others improve in their perseverance or resilience?

3. *Rise Up*

    a. This week, how have you shown confidence, courage, and/or humility?

    b. What can you do in the week ahead to work on and improve in these areas?

4. *Keeping Score*

    a. This week, what have you done to hold yourself or others accountable?

b. What are some areas in the week ahead where you can do a better job of keeping score?

_____

_____

_____

c. Have you checked in with your accountability partner(s) lately?

_____

_____

_____

5. *Huddle*

a. This week, what have you done to build your team or improve teamwork personally and/ or professionally?

_____

_____

_____

b. How can you improve on or strengthen the teams you are a part of, this coming week?

_____

_____

_____

6. *Fierce*

a. Over the past week when have you demonstrated assertiveness, aggressiveness, or competitiveness?

_____

_____

_____

b. Next week, what can you do to use these qualities to your advantage?

_____

_____

_____

_____

7. *Triumph*

a. How have you demonstrated leadership qualities this week?

_____

_____

_____

_____

b. What can you do to improve or enhance your leadership skills in the coming week and better execute your game plan?

_____

_____

_____

_____

Using concepts that you learned from reading each principle, evaluate where you are at with these areas. Incorporate visualizations to support what you want to see yourself doing and how it feels to have accomplished them.

You are deserving of your triumph! Now it's time to start working to create it.

Take a few deep breaths, visualize and see this in the present moment completed.

Date: / /

The Pessimist Sees Difficulty In Every Opportunity. The Optimist Sees Opportunity In Every Difficulty. —Winston Churchill

I am grateful for:

1. _____
2. _____
3. _____

My commitments today:

1. _____
2. _____

My daily push mindset:

1. _____

_____

_____

_____

_____

_____

_____

Date: ___/___/_____

Anything in life worth having is worth working for.
—Andrew Carnegie

I am grateful for:

1. _____
2. _____
3. _____

My commitments today:

1. _____
2. _____

My daily push mindset:

1. _____

_____

_____

_____

_____

_____

_____

Date: ___/___/___

Most of the important things in the world have been accomplished by people who have kept on trying when there seemed to be no hope at all. —Dale Carnegie

I am grateful for:

1. _____
2. _____
3. _____

My commitments today:

1. _____
2. _____

My daily push mindset:

1. _____
_____
_____
_____
_____
_____

Date: ___/___/_____

Our greatest glory is not in never falling, but in rising every time we fall. —Confucius

I am grateful for:

1. _____
2. _____
3. _____

My commitments today:

1. _____
2. _____

My daily push mindset:

1. _____

_____

_____

_____

_____

_____

_____

Date: ___/___/_____

Success is never ending, failure is never final.
—Dr. Robert Schuller

I am grateful for:

1. _____
2. _____
3. _____

My commitments today:

1. _____
2. _____

My daily push mindset:

1. _____

_____

_____

_____

_____

_____

_____

Date: ___/___/_____

I just love when people say I can't do something because all my life people said I wasn't going to make it. —Ted Turner

I am grateful for:

1. _____
2. _____
3. _____

My commitments today:

1. _____
2. _____

My daily push mindset:

1. _____

_____

_____

_____

_____

_____

_____

Weekly Reflection for My Daily Push Journal

We also want you to commit to 100% participation in this reflection once a week.

The guidelines to give you the best success are:

1. Find a quiet place that is technology- and people-free (aside from music that may lend to focus)

2. Do not rush, stay present, enjoy the journey

3. Find takeaways from each area of evaluation (what you learned, what you need to improve on, what is working, etc.)

Everyone has a way to give this amount of time to their success every week.

Topic to reflect on:

1. *Practice, Practice, Practice*

   a. What areas in the last week have you shown discipline, outlined a routine, or demonstrated strong time management?

   b. What areas in the last week need improvement or more practice in the week ahead?

2. *Just Keep Going*

   a. In the last week, how have you demonstrated perseverance or resilience?

_____

_____

_____

   b. What can you do in the week ahead to improve and/or help others improve in their perseverance or resilience?

_____

_____

_____

3. *Rise Up*

   a. This week, how have you shown confidence, courage, and/or humility?

_____

_____

_____

   b. What can you do in the week ahead to work on and improve in these areas?

_____

_____

_____

4. *Keeping Score*

   a. This week, what have you done to hold yourself or others accountable?

_____

_____

_____

b. What are some areas in the week ahead where you can do a better job of keeping score?

c. Have you checked in with your accountability partner(s) lately?

5. *Huddle*

a. This week, what have you done to build your team or improve teamwork personally and/ or professionally?

b. How can you improve on or strengthen the teams you are a part of, this coming week?

6. *Fierce*

a. Over the past week when have you demonstrated assertiveness, aggressiveness, or competitiveness?

b. Next week, what can you do to use these qualities to your advantage?

_____

_____

_____

_____

7. *Triumph*

   a. How have you demonstrated leadership qualities this week?

_____

_____

_____

_____

   b. What can you do to improve or enhance your leadership skills in the coming week and better execute your game plan?

_____

_____

_____

_____

Using concepts that you learned from reading each principle, evaluate where you are at with these areas. Incorporate visualizations to support what you want to see yourself doing and how it feels to have accomplished them.

You are deserving of your triumph! Now it's time to start working to create it.

Take a few deep breaths, visualize and see this in the present moment completed.

Date: ___ / ___ / _____

Obstacles are those frightful things you can see when you take your eyes off your goal. —Henry Ford

I am grateful for:

1. _____
2. _____
3. _____

My commitments today:

1. _____
2. _____

My daily push mindset:

1. _____

_____

_____

_____

_____

_____

Date: ___/___/___

It takes a strong fish to swim against the current. Even a dead one can float with it. —John Crowe

I am grateful for:

1. _____
2. _____
3. _____

My commitments today:

1. _____
2. _____

My daily push mindset:

1. _____

_____

_____

_____

_____

_____

Date: ___/___/_____

You will never find time for anything. You must make it.
—Charles Buxton

I am grateful for:

1. _____
2. _____
3. _____

My commitments today:

1. _____
2. _____

My daily push mindset:

1. _____

_____

_____

_____

_____

_____

_____

Date: ___/___/_____

Remove failure as an option. —Joan Lunden

I am grateful for:

1. _____
2. _____
3. _____

My commitments today:

1. _____
2. _____

My daily push mindset:

1. _____

_____

_____

_____

_____

_____

_____

Date: ___ / ___ / _____

There is no one giant step that does it. It's a lot of little steps.
—Peter A. Cohen

I am grateful for:

1. _____
2. _____
3. _____

My commitments today:

1. _____
2. _____

My daily push mindset:

1. _____

_____

_____

_____

_____

_____

_____

Date: ___ / ___ / ___

Shoot for the moon. Even if you miss, you will land among the stars. —Les Brown

I am grateful for:

1. _____
2. _____
3. _____

My commitments today:

1. _____
2. _____

My daily push mindset:

1. _____

_____

_____

_____

_____

_____

_____

Weekly Reflection for My Daily Push Journal

We also want you to commit to 100% participation in this reflection once a week.

The guidelines to give you the best success are:

1. Find a quiet place that is technology- and people-free (aside from music that may lend to focus)

2. Do not rush, stay present, enjoy the journey

3. Find takeaways from each area of evaluation (what you learned, what you need to improve on, what is working, etc.)

Everyone has a way to give this amount of time to their success every week.

Topic to reflect on:

1. *Practice, Practice, Practice*

   a. What areas in the last week have you shown discipline, outlined a routine, or demonstrated strong time management?

   _____

   _____

   _____

   b. What areas in the last week need improvement or more practice in the week ahead?

   _____

   _____

   _____

2. *Just Keep Going*

    a. In the last week, how have you demonstrated perseverance or resilience?

    b. What can you do in the week ahead to improve and/or help others improve in their perseverance or resilience?

3. *Rise Up*

    a. This week, how have you shown confidence, courage, and/or humility?

    b. What can you do in the week ahead to work on and improve in these areas?

4. *Keeping Score*

    a. This week, what have you done to hold yourself or others accountable?

b. What are some areas in the week ahead where you can do a better job of keeping score?

c. Have you checked in with your accountability partner(s) lately?

5. *Huddle*

   a. This week, what have you done to build your team or improve teamwork personally and/ or professionally?

   b. How can you improve on or strengthen the teams you are a part of, this coming week?

6. *Fierce*

   a. Over the past week when have you demonstrated assertiveness, aggressiveness, or competitiveness?

b. Next week, what can you do to use these qualities to your advantage?

-----

7. *Triumph*

a. How have you demonstrated leadership qualities this week?

-----

b. What can you do to improve or enhance your leadership skills in the coming week and better execute your game plan?

Using concepts that you learned from reading each principle, evaluate where you are at with these areas. Incorporate visualizations to support what you want to see yourself doing and how it feels to have accomplished them.

You are deserving of your triumph! Now it's time to start working to create it.

Take a few deep breaths, visualize and see this in the present moment completed.

Date: ___/___/___

Some of us have great runways already built for us. If you have one, take off. But if you don't have one, realize it is your responsibility to grab a shovel and build one for yourself and for those who will follow after you. —Amelia Earhart

I am grateful for:

1. _____
2. _____
3. _____

My commitments today:

1. _____
2. _____

My daily push mindset:

1. _____

_____

_____

_____

_____

_____

Date: ___/___/_____

Work like you don't need the money. Love like you've never been hurt. Dance like nobody is watching. —Mark Twain

I am grateful for:

1. _____
2. _____
3. _____

My commitments today:

1. _____
2. _____

My daily push mindset:

1. _____

_____

_____

_____

_____

_____

_____

Date: ___/___/___

What the mind of man can conceive and believe, it can achieve. —Napoleon Hill

I am grateful for:

1. _____
2. _____
3. _____

My commitments today:

1. _____
2. _____

My daily push mindset:

1. _____
_____
_____
_____
_____
_____
_____

Date: ___/___/___

There are no secrets to success. It is the result of preparation, hard work, and learning from failure. —Colin Powell

I am grateful for:

1. _____
2. _____
3. _____

My commitments today:

1. _____
2. _____

My daily push mindset:

1. _____
_____
_____
_____
_____
_____
_____

Date: / /

What lies behind us and what lies before us are tiny matters compared to what lies within us. —Ralph Waldo Emerson

I am grateful for:

1. _____
2. _____
3. _____

My commitments today:

1. _____
2. _____

My daily push mindset:

1. _____

_____

_____

_____

_____

_____

Date: ___/___/_____

Great works are performed not by strength but by perseverance.
—Samuel Johnson

I am grateful for:

1. _____
2. _____
3. _____

My commitments today:

1. _____
2. _____

My daily push mindset:

1. _____
_____
_____
_____
_____
_____
_____

Weekly Reflection for My Daily Push Journal

We also want you to commit to 100% participation in this reflection once a week.

The guidelines to give you the best success are:

1. Find a quiet place that is technology- and people-free (aside from music that may lend to focus)

2. Do not rush, stay present, enjoy the journey

3. Find takeaways from each area of evaluation (what you learned, what you need to improve on, what is working, etc.)

Everyone has a way to give this amount of time to their success every week.

Topic to reflect on:

1. *Practice, Practice, Practice*

   a. What areas in the last week have you shown discipline, outlined a routine, or demonstrated strong time management?

   _____

   _____

   b. What areas in the last week need improvement or more practice in the week ahead?

   _____

   _____

2. *Just Keep Going*

    a. In the last week, how have you demonstrated perseverance or resilience?

_____

_____

_____

    b. What can you do in the week ahead to improve and/or help others improve in their perseverance or resilience?

_____

_____

_____

3. *Rise Up*

    a. This week, how have you shown confidence, courage, and/or humility?

_____

_____

_____

    b. What can you do in the week ahead to work on and improve in these areas?

_____

_____

_____

4. *Keeping Score*

    a. This week, what have you done to hold yourself or others accountable?

_____

_____

_____

b. What are some areas in the week ahead where you can do a better job of keeping score?

c. Have you checked in with your accountability partner(s) lately?

5. *Huddle*

a. This week, what have you done to build your team or improve teamwork personally and/ or professionally?

b. How can you improve on or strengthen the teams you are a part of, this coming week?

6. *Fierce*

a. Over the past week when have you demonstrated assertiveness, aggressiveness, or competitiveness?

b. Next week, what can you do to use these qualities to your advantage?

_____

_____

_____

_____

7. *Triumph*

a. How have you demonstrated leadership qualities this week?

_____

_____

_____

_____

b. What can you do to improve or enhance your leadership skills in the coming week and better execute your game plan?

_____

_____

_____

_____

Using concepts that you learned from reading each principle, evaluate where you are at with these areas. Incorporate visualizations to support what you want to see yourself doing and how it feels to have accomplished them.

You are deserving of your triumph! Now it's time to start working to create it.

Take a few deep breaths, visualize and see this in the present moment completed.

Date: ___/___/_____

The difference between a successful person and others is not a lack of strength, not a lack of knowledge, but rather a lack of will.
—Vince Lombardi

I am grateful for:

1. _____
2. _____
3. _____

My commitments today:

1. _____
2. _____

My daily push mindset:

1. _____
_____
_____
_____
_____
_____
_____

Date: ___ / ___ / _____

The man who follows the crowd will usually get no further than the crowd. The man who walks alone is likely to find himself in places no one has ever been. —Alan Ashley-Pitt

I am grateful for:

1. _____
2. _____
3. _____

My commitments today:

1. _____
2. _____

My daily push mindset:

1. _____

_____

_____

_____

_____

_____

_____

Date: ___/___/_____

It takes 20 years to build a reputation and five minutes to ruin it. If you think about that, you'll do things differently.
—Warren Buffett

I am grateful for:

1. _____
2. _____
3. _____

My commitments today:

1. _____
2. _____

My daily push mindset:

1. _____
_____
_____
_____
_____
_____
_____
_____

Date: ____/____/_____

> *Champions aren't made in the gyms. Champions are made from something they have deep inside them —a desire, a dream, a vision.* —Muhammad Ali

I am grateful for:

1. _____
2. _____
3. _____

My commitments today:

1. _____
2. _____

My daily push mindset:

1. _____

_____

_____

_____

_____

_____

_____

Date: ___ / ___ / ___

Whatever you vividly imagine, ardently desire, sincerely believe, and enthusiastically act upon must inevitably come to pass! —Paul J. Meyer

I am grateful for:

1. _____
2. _____
3. _____

My commitments today:

1. _____
2. _____

My daily push mindset:

1. _____

_____

_____

_____

_____

_____

_____

Date: ___/___/___

Keep away from small people who try to belittle your ambitions. Small people always do that, but the really great make you feel that you too can become great. —Mark Twain

I am grateful for:

1. _____
2. _____
3. _____

My commitments today:

1. _____
2. _____

My daily push mindset:

1. _____
_____
_____
_____
_____
_____
_____

WEEKLY REFLECTION FOR MY DAILY PUSH JOURNAL

We also want you to commit to 100% participation in this reflection once a week.

The guidelines to give you the best success are:

1. Find a quiet place that is technology- and people-free (aside from music that may lend to focus)

2. Do not rush, stay present, enjoy the journey

3. Find takeaways from each area of evaluation (what you learned, what you need to improve on, what is working, etc.)

Everyone has a way to give this amount of time to their success every week.

Topic to reflect on:

1. *Practice, Practice, Practice*

   a. What areas in the last week have you shown discipline, outlined a routine, or demonstrated strong time management?

   b. What areas in the last week need improvement or more practice in the week ahead?

2. *Just Keep Going*

   a. In the last week, how have you demonstrated perseverance or resilience?

   b. What can you do in the week ahead to improve and/or help others improve in their perseverance or resilience?

3. *Rise Up*

   a. This week, how have you shown confidence, courage, and/or humility?

   b. What can you do in the week ahead to work on and improve in these areas?

4. *Keeping Score*

   a. This week, what have you done to hold yourself or others accountable?

b. What are some areas in the week ahead where you can do a better job of keeping score?

c. Have you checked in with your accountability partner(s) lately?

5. *Huddle*

a. This week, what have you done to build your team or improve teamwork personally and/ or professionally?

b. How can you improve on or strengthen the teams you are a part of, this coming week?

6. *Fierce*

a. Over the past week when have you demonstrated assertiveness, aggressiveness, or competitiveness?

b. Next week, what can you do to use these qualities to your advantage?

_____

_____

_____

_____

7. *Triumph*

a. How have you demonstrated leadership qualities this week?

_____

_____

_____

_____

b. What can you do to improve or enhance your leadership skills in the coming week and better execute your game plan?

_____

_____

_____

_____

Using concepts that you learned from reading each principle, evaluate where you are at with these areas. Incorporate visualizations to support what you want to see yourself doing and how it feels to have accomplished them.

You are deserving of your triumph! Now it's time to start working to create it.

Take a few deep breaths, visualize and see this in the present moment completed.

Date: ___/___/_____

For anything worth having one must pay the price; and the price is always work, patience, love, self-sacrifice. No paper currency, no promises to pay, but the gold of real service.
— John Burroughs

I am grateful for:

1. _____
2. _____
3. _____

My commitments today:

1. _____
2. _____

My daily push mindset:

1. _____

_____

_____

_____

_____

_____

Date: ___/___/_____

To be successful, you must decide exactly what you want to accomplish, then resolve to pay the price to get it.
                                                    —Bunker Hunt

I am grateful for:

1. _____
2. _____
3. _____

My commitments today:

1. _____
2. _____

My daily push mindset:

1. _____

_____

_____

_____

_____

_____

_____

Date: ___ / ___ / ___

You just can't beat the person who never gives up.
—Babe Ruth

I am grateful for:

1. _____
2. _____
3. _____

My commitments today:

1. _____
2. _____

My daily push mindset:

1. _____

_____

_____

_____

_____

_____

_____

Date: ___/___/_____

When you get right down to the root of the meaning of the word 'succeed', you find it simply means to follow through.

—F.W. Nichol

I am grateful for:

1. _____
2. _____
3. _____

My commitments today:

1. _____
2. _____

My daily push mindset:

1. _____

_____

_____

_____

_____

_____

_____

MY DAILY PUSH JOURNAL

Date: _/_/_

Successful people are always looking for opportunities to help others. Unsuccessful people are always asking, 'What's in it for me?' —Brian Tracy

I am grateful for:

1. _____
2. _____
3. _____

My commitments today:

1. _____
2. _____

My daily push mindset:

1. _____
_____
_____
_____
_____
_____
_____

Date: ___ / ___ / ___

If you don't set goals, you can't regret not reaching them.
—Yogi Berra

I am grateful for:

1. _____
2. _____
3. _____

My commitments today:

1. _____
2. _____

My daily push mindset:

1. _____

_____

_____

_____

_____

_____

_____

Weekly Reflection for My Daily Push Journal

We also want you to commit to 100% participation in this reflection once a week.

The guidelines to give you the best success are:

1. Find a quiet place that is technology- and people-free (aside from music that may lend to focus)

2. Do not rush, stay present, enjoy the journey

3. Find takeaways from each area of evaluation (what you learned, what you need to improve on, what is working, etc.)

Everyone has a way to give this amount of time to their success every week.

Topic to reflect on:

1. *Practice, Practice, Practice*

   a. What areas in the last week have you shown discipline, outlined a routine, or demonstrated strong time management?

   b. What areas in the last week need improvement or more practice in the week ahead?

2. *Just Keep Going*

   a. In the last week, how have you demonstrated perseverance or resilience?

   b. What can you do in the week ahead to improve and/or help others improve in their perseverance or resilience?

3. *Rise Up*

   a. This week, how have you shown confidence, courage, and/or humility?

   b. What can you do in the week ahead to work on and improve in these areas?

4. *Keeping Score*

   a. This week, what have you done to hold yourself or others accountable?

b. What are some areas in the week ahead where you can do a better job of keeping score?

c. Have you checked in with your accountability partner(s) lately?

5. *Huddle*

a. This week, what have you done to build your team or improve teamwork personally and/ or professionally?

b. How can you improve on or strengthen the teams you are a part of, this coming week?

6. *Fierce*

a. Over the past week when have you demonstrated assertiveness, aggressiveness, or competitiveness?

b. Next week, what can you do to use these qualities to your advantage?

_____

_____

_____

_____

7. *Triumph*

a. How have you demonstrated leadership qualities this week?

_____

_____

_____

_____

b. What can you do to improve or enhance your leadership skills in the coming week and better execute your game plan?

_____

_____

_____

_____

Using concepts that you learned from reading each principle, evaluate where you are at with these areas. Incorporate visualizations to support what you want to see yourself doing and how it feels to have accomplished them.

You are deserving of your triumph! Now it's time to start working to create it.

Take a few deep breaths, visualize and see this in the present moment completed.

Date: ___/___/_____

*Success is achieved by those who try and keep trying with a
positive mental attitude.* —W. Clement Stone

I am grateful for:

1. _____
2. _____
3. _____

My commitments today:

1. _____
2. _____

My daily push mindset:

1. _____

_____

_____

_____

_____

_____

_____

Date: ___/___/_____

I couldn't wait for success, so I went ahead without it.
—Jonathan Winters

I am grateful for:

1. _____
2. _____
3. _____

My commitments today:

1. _____
2. _____

My daily push mindset:

1. _____

_____

_____

_____

_____

_____

_____

Date: ___/___/_____

What we hope to do with ease, we must learn first to do with diligence. —Samuel Johnson

I am grateful for:

1. _____
2. _____
3. _____

My commitments today:

1. _____
2. _____

My daily push mindset:

1. _____
_____
_____
_____
_____
_____
_____

Date: ___/___/_____

We do our best that we know how at the moment, and if it doesn't turn out, we modify it. —Franklin Delano Roosevelt

I am grateful for:

1. _____
2. _____
3. _____

My commitments today:

1. _____
2. _____

My daily push mindset:

1. _____

_____

_____

_____

_____

_____

Date: ___/___/_____

Enthusiasm is the steam that drives the engine.

—Napoleon Hill

I am grateful for:

1. _____
2. _____
3. _____

My commitments today:

1. _____
2. _____

My daily push mindset:

1. _____

_____

_____

_____

_____

_____

_____

Date: ___/___/___

Success in life has nothing to do with what you gain in life or accomplish for yourself. It's what you do for others.

—Danny Thomas

I am grateful for:

1. _____
2. _____
3. _____

My commitments today:

1. _____
2. _____

My daily push mindset:

1. _____

_____

_____

_____

_____

_____

_____

Weekly Reflection for My Daily Push Journal

We also want you to commit to 100% participation in this reflection once a week.

The guidelines to give you the best success are:

1. Find a quiet place that is technology- and people-free (aside from music that may lend to focus)

2. Do not rush, stay present, enjoy the journey

3. Find takeaways from each area of evaluation (what you learned, what you need to improve on, what is working, etc.)

Everyone has a way to give this amount of time to their success every week.

Topic to reflect on:

1. *Practice, Practice, Practice*

   a. What areas in the last week have you shown discipline, outlined a routine, or demonstrated strong time management?

   b. What areas in the last week need improvement or more practice in the week ahead?

2. *Just Keep Going*

    a. In the last week, how have you demonstrated perseverance or resilience?

_____

_____

_____

    b. What can you do in the week ahead to improve and/or help others improve in their perseverance or resilience?

_____

_____

_____

3. *Rise Up*

    a. This week, how have you shown confidence, courage, and/or humility?

_____

_____

_____

    b. What can you do in the week ahead to work on and improve in these areas?

_____

_____

_____

4. *Keeping Score*

    a. This week, what have you done to hold yourself or others accountable?

_____

_____

_____

b. What are some areas in the week ahead where you can do a better job of keeping score?

c. Have you checked in with your accountability partner(s) lately?

5. *Huddle*

a. This week, what have you done to build your team or improve teamwork personally and/ or professionally?

b. How can you improve on or strengthen the teams you are a part of, this coming week?

6. *Fierce*

a. Over the past week when have you demonstrated assertiveness, aggressiveness, or competitiveness?

b. Next week, what can you do to use these qualities to your advantage?

_____

_____

_____

_____

7. *Triumph*

a. How have you demonstrated leadership qualities this week?

_____

_____

_____

_____

b. What can you do to improve or enhance your leadership skills in the coming week and better execute your game plan?

_____

_____

_____

_____

Using concepts that you learned from reading each principle, evaluate where you are at with these areas. Incorporate visualizations to support what you want to see yourself doing and how it feels to have accomplished them.

You are deserving of your triumph! Now it's time to start working to create it.

Take a few deep breaths, visualize and see this in the present moment completed.

Date: ___/___/___

Empty pockets never held anyone back. Only empty heads and empty hearts can do that. —Norman Vincent Peale

I am grateful for:

1. _____
2. _____
3. _____

My commitments today:

1. _____
2. _____

My daily push mindset:

1. _____

_____

_____

_____

_____

_____

_____

Date: ___ / ___ / ___

One man with courage is a majority. —Andrew Jackson

I am grateful for:

1. _____
2. _____
3. _____

My commitments today:

1. _____
2. _____

My daily push mindset:

1. _____

_____

_____

_____

_____

_____

_____

Date: ___/___/_____

Every achiever I have ever met says, 'My life turned around when I began to believe in me.'
—Robert Schuller

I am grateful for:

1. _____
2. _____
3. _____

My commitments today:

1. _____
2. _____

My daily push mindset:

1. _____

_____

_____

_____

_____

_____

_____

Date: ___/___/_____

I don't measure a man's success by how high he climbs but how high he bounces when he hits bottom. —George Patton

I am grateful for:

1. _____
2. _____
3. _____

My commitments today:

1. _____
2. _____

My daily push mindset:

1. _____

_____

_____

_____

_____

_____

_____

Date: / /

One step —choosing a goal and sticking to it —changes everything. —Scott Reed

I am grateful for:

1.
2.
3.

My commitments today:

1.
2.

My daily push mindset:

1.

Date: ___/___/_____

I don't know what your destiny will be, but one thing I do know: The only ones among you who will be really happy are those who have sought and found how to serve.

—Albert Schweitzer

I am grateful for:

1. _____
2. _____
3. _____

My commitments today:

1. _____
2. _____

My daily push mindset:

1. _____

_____

_____

_____

_____

_____

_____

We also want you to commit to 100% participation in this reflection once a week.

The guidelines to give you the best success are:

1. Find a quiet place that is technology- and people-free (aside from music that may lend to focus)

2. Do not rush, stay present, enjoy the journey

3. Find takeaways from each area of evaluation (what you learned, what you need to improve on, what is working, etc.)

Everyone has a way to give this amount of time to their success every week.

Topic to reflect on:

1. *Practice, Practice, Practice*

   a. What areas in the last week have you shown discipline, outlined a routine, or demonstrated strong time management?

   ....

   ....

   b. What areas in the last week need improvement or more practice in the week ahead?

   ....

   ....

   ....

2. *Just Keep Going*

a. In the last week, how have you demonstrated perseverance or resilience?

_____

_____

_____

b. What can you do in the week ahead to improve and/or help others improve in their perseverance or resilience?

_____

_____

_____

3. *Rise Up*

a. This week, how have you shown confidence, courage, and/or humility?

_____

_____

_____

b. What can you do in the week ahead to work on and improve in these areas?

_____

_____

_____

4. *Keeping Score*

a. This week, what have you done to hold yourself or others accountable?

_____

_____

_____

b. What are some areas in the week ahead where you can do a better job of keeping score?

c. Have you checked in with your accountability partner(s) lately?

5. *Huddle*

  a. This week, what have you done to build your team or improve teamwork personally and/ or professionally?

  b. How can you improve on or strengthen the teams you are a part of, this coming week?

6. *Fierce*

  a. Over the past week when have you demonstrated assertiveness, aggressiveness, or competitiveness?

b. Next week, what can you do to use these qualities to your advantage?

----

7. *Triumph*

a. How have you demonstrated leadership qualities this week?

----

b. What can you do to improve or enhance your leadership skills in the coming week and better execute your game plan?

Using concepts that you learned from reading each principle, evaluate where you are at with these areas. Incorporate visualizations to support what you want to see yourself doing and how it feels to have accomplished them.

You are deserving of your triumph! Now it's time to start working to create it.

Take a few deep breaths, visualize and see this in the present moment completed.

Date: ___ / ___ / ___

Success is the child of audacity. —Benjamin Disraeli

I am grateful for:

1. _____
2. _____
3. _____

My commitments today:

1. _____
2. _____

My daily push mindset:

1. _____

_____

_____

_____

_____

_____

_____

Date: ___/___/_____

Teamwork is the long word for success.

—Jacquelinemae A. Rudd

I am grateful for:

1. _____
2. _____
3. _____

My commitments today:

1. _____
2. _____

My daily push mindset:

1. _____

_____

_____

_____

_____

_____

_____

Date: ___ / ___ / _____

Except and expect positive things and that is what you will receive. —Lori Hard

I am grateful for:

1. _____
2. _____
3. _____

My commitments today:

1. _____
2. _____

My daily push mindset:

1. _____

_____

_____

_____

_____

_____

_____

Date: ___/___/_____

When you come to the end of your rope, tie a knot and hang on. —Franklin D. Roosevelt

I am grateful for:

1. _____
2. _____
3. _____

My commitments today:

1. _____
2. _____

My daily push mindset:

1. _____

_____

_____

_____

_____

_____

_____

Date: ___/___/_____

You measure the size of the accomplishment by the
obstacles you had to overcome to reach your goals.
—Booker T. Washington

I am grateful for:

1. _____
2. _____
3. _____

My commitments today:

1. _____
2. _____

My daily push mindset:

1. _____
_____
_____
_____
_____
_____
_____

Date: ___/___/___

In order to succeed you must fail so that you know what not to do the next time. —Anthony J. D'Angelo

I am grateful for:

1. _____
2. _____
3. _____

My commitments today:

1. _____
2. _____

My daily push mindset:

1. _____

_____

_____

_____

_____

_____

_____

Weekly Reflection for My Daily Push Journal

We also want you to commit to 100% participation in this reflection once a week.

The guidelines to give you the best success are:

1. Find a quiet place that is technology- and people-free (aside from music that may lend to focus)

2. Do not rush, stay present, enjoy the journey

3. Find takeaways from each area of evaluation (what you learned, what you need to improve on, what is working, etc.)

Everyone has a way to give this amount of time to their success every week.

Topic to reflect on:

1. *Practice, Practice, Practice*

   a. What areas in the last week have you shown discipline, outlined a routine, or demonstrated strong time management?

   _____

   _____

   _____

   b. What areas in the last week need improvement or more practice in the week ahead?

   _____

   _____

   _____

2. *Just Keep Going*

   a. In the last week, how have you demonstrated perseverance or resilience?

   _____

   _____

   _____

   b. What can you do in the week ahead to improve and/or help others improve in their perseverance or resilience?

   _____

   _____

   _____

3. *Rise Up*

   a. This week, how have you shown confidence, courage, and/or humility?

   _____

   _____

   _____

   b. What can you do in the week ahead to work on and improve in these areas?

   _____

   _____

   _____

4. *Keeping Score*

   a. This week, what have you done to hold yourself or others accountable?

   _____

   _____

   _____

b. What are some areas in the week ahead where you can do a better job of keeping score?

_____

_____

_____

c. Have you checked in with your accountability partner(s) lately?

_____

_____

_____

5. *Huddle*

a. This week, what have you done to build your team or improve teamwork personally and/ or professionally?

_____

_____

_____

b. How can you improve on or strengthen the teams you are a part of, this coming week?

_____

_____

_____

6. *Fierce*

a. Over the past week when have you demonstrated assertiveness, aggressiveness, or competitiveness?

_____

_____

_____

b. Next week, what can you do to use these qualities to your advantage?

7. *Triumph*

a. How have you demonstrated leadership qualities this week?

b. What can you do to improve or enhance your leadership skills in the coming week and better execute your game plan?

Using concepts that you learned from reading each principle, evaluate where you are at with these areas. Incorporate visualizations to support what you want to see yourself doing and how it feels to have accomplished them.

You are deserving of your triumph! Now it's time to start working to create it.

Take a few deep breaths, visualize and see this in the present moment completed.

Date: ___ / ___ / ___

Those at the top of the mountain didn't fall there.
—Marcus Washling

I am grateful for:

1. _____
2. _____
3. _____

My commitments today:

1. _____
2. _____

My daily push mindset:

1. _____

_____

_____

_____

_____

_____

_____

Date: ___/___/___

Motivation is what gets you started. Habit is what keeps you going! —Jim Ryun

I am grateful for:

1. _____
2. _____
3. _____

My commitments today:

1. _____
2. _____

My daily push mindset:

1. _____

_____

_____

_____

_____

_____

Date: ___/___/_____

The successful man will profit from his mistakes and try again in a different way. —Dale Carnegie

I am grateful for:

1. _____
2. _____
3. _____

My commitments today:

1. _____
2. _____

My daily push mindset:

1. _____

_____

_____

_____

_____

_____

Date: ___/___/_____

Only those who risk going too far can possibly find out how far one can go. —T.S. Eliot

I am grateful for:

1. _____
2. _____
3. _____

My commitments today:

1. _____
2. _____

My daily push mindset:

1. _____

_____

_____

_____

_____

_____

_____

Date: ___ / ___ / ___

It's amazing what ordinary people can do if they set out without preconceived notions. —Charles F. Kettering

I am grateful for:

1. _____
2. _____
3. _____

My commitments today:

1. _____
2. _____

My daily push mindset:

1. _____

_____

_____

_____

_____

_____

Date: ___ / ___ / ___

People who are afraid to fail can never experience the joys of success. —Pete Zafra

I am grateful for:

1. _____
2. _____
3. _____

My commitments today:

1. _____
2. _____

My daily push mindset:

1. _____

_____

_____

_____

_____

_____

_____

WEEKLY REFLECTION FOR MY DAILY PUSH JOURNAL

We also want you to commit to 100% participation in this reflection once a week.

The guidelines to give you the best success are:

1. Find a quiet place that is technology- and people-free (aside from music that may lend to focus)

2. Do not rush, stay present, enjoy the journey

3. Find takeaways from each area of evaluation (what you learned, what you need to improve on, what is working, etc.)

Everyone has a way to give this amount of time to their success every week.

Topic to reflect on:

1. *Practice, Practice, Practice*

   a. What areas in the last week have you shown discipline, outlined a routine, or demonstrated strong time management?

   b. What areas in the last week need improvement or more practice in the week ahead?

2. *Just Keep Going*

    a. In the last week, how have you demonstrated perseverance or resilience?

    b. What can you do in the week ahead to improve and/or help others improve in their perseverance or resilience?

3. *Rise Up*

    a. This week, how have you shown confidence, courage, and/or humility?

    b. What can you do in the week ahead to work on and improve in these areas?

4. *Keeping Score*

    a. This week, what have you done to hold yourself or others accountable?

b. What are some areas in the week ahead where you can do a better job of keeping score?

_____

_____

_____

c. Have you checked in with your accountability partner(s) lately?

_____

_____

_____

5. *Huddle*

a. This week, what have you done to build your team or improve teamwork personally and/ or professionally?

_____

_____

_____

b. How can you improve on or strengthen the teams you are a part of, this coming week?

_____

_____

_____

6. *Fierce*

a. Over the past week when have you demonstrated assertiveness, aggressiveness, or competitiveness?

_____

_____

_____

b. Next week, what can you do to use these qualities to your advantage?

7. *Triumph*

a. How have you demonstrated leadership qualities this week?

b. What can you do to improve or enhance your leadership skills in the coming week and better execute your game plan?

Using concepts that you learned from reading each principle, evaluate where you are at with these areas. Incorporate visualizations to support what you want to see yourself doing and how it feels to have accomplished them.

You are deserving of your triumph! Now it's time to start working to create it.

Take a few deep breaths, visualize and see this in the present moment completed.

Date: ___/___/_____

No matter how small, acknowledge the achievement.
—Greg Henry Quinn

I am grateful for:

1. _____
2. _____
3. _____

My commitments today:

1. _____
2. _____

My daily push mindset:

1. _____

_____

_____

_____

_____

_____

_____

Date: ___ / ___ / _____

If you don't quit, and don't cheat, and don't run home when trouble arrives, you can only win. —Shelley Long

I am grateful for:

1. _____
2. _____
3. _____

My commitments today:

1. _____
2. _____

My daily push mindset:

1. _____

_____

_____

_____

_____

_____

Date: ___/___/___

Put your heart, mind, intellect, and soul even to your smallest acts. This is the secret of success. —Swami Sivananda

I am grateful for:

1. _____
2. _____
3. _____

My commitments today:

1. _____
2. _____

My daily push mindset:

1. _____

_____

_____

_____

_____

_____

Date: ___/___/_____

The person who makes a success of living is the one who sees his goal steadily and aims for it unswervingly. That is dedication.
—Cecil B. DeMille

I am grateful for:

1. _____
2. _____
3. _____

My commitments today:

1. _____
2. _____

My daily push mindset:

1. _____

_____

_____

_____

_____

_____

_____

Date: ___ / ___ / ___

It is in the small decisions you and I make every day that create our destiny. —Anthony Robbins

I am grateful for:

1. _____
2. _____
3. _____

My commitments today:

1. _____
2. _____

My daily push mindset:

1. _____
_____
_____
_____
_____
_____
_____

Date: ___/___/___

Life is not easy for any of us, but what of that? We must have perseverance and above all confidence in ourselves.

—Marie Curie

I am grateful for:

1. _____

2. _____

3. _____

My commitments today:

1. _____

2. _____

My daily push mindset:

1. _____

_____

_____

_____

_____

_____

_____

Weekly Reflection for My Daily Push Journal

We also want you to commit to 100% participation in this reflection once a week.

The guidelines to give you the best success are:

1. Find a quiet place that is technology- and people-free (aside from music that may lend to focus)

2. Do not rush, stay present, enjoy the journey

3. Find takeaways from each area of evaluation (what you learned, what you need to improve on, what is working, etc.)

Everyone has a way to give this amount of time to their success every week.

Topic to reflect on:

1. *Practice, Practice, Practice*

   a. What areas in the last week have you shown discipline, outlined a routine, or demonstrated strong time management?

   _____

   _____

   _____

   b. What areas in the last week need improvement or more practice in the week ahead?

   _____

   _____

   _____

2. *Just Keep Going*

   a. In the last week, how have you demonstrated perseverance or resilience?

   b. What can you do in the week ahead to improve and/or help others improve in their perseverance or resilience?

3. *Rise Up*

   a. This week, how have you shown confidence, courage, and/or humility?

   b. What can you do in the week ahead to work on and improve in these areas?

4. *Keeping Score*

   a. This week, what have you done to hold yourself or others accountable?

b. What are some areas in the week ahead where you can do a better job of keeping score?

c. Have you checked in with your accountability partner(s) lately?

5. *Huddle*

a. This week, what have you done to build your team or improve teamwork personally and/ or professionally?

b. How can you improve on or strengthen the teams you are a part of, this coming week?

6. *Fierce*

a. Over the past week when have you demonstrated assertiveness, aggressiveness, or competitiveness?

b. Next week, what can you do to use these qualities to your advantage?

_____

_____

_____

_____

7. *Triumph*

   a. How have you demonstrated leadership qualities this week?

_____

_____

_____

_____

   b. What can you do to improve or enhance your leadership skills in the coming week and better execute your game plan?

_____

_____

_____

_____

Using concepts that you learned from reading each principle, evaluate where you are at with these areas. Incorporate visualizations to support what you want to see yourself doing and how it feels to have accomplished them.

You are deserving of your triumph! Now it's time to start working to create it.

Take a few deep breaths, visualize and see this in the present moment completed.

Date: ___ / ___ / ___

There are two primary choices in life: to accept conditions as they exist, or accept the responsibility for changing them.
—Denis Waitley

I am grateful for:

1. _____
2. _____
3. _____

My commitments today:

1. _____
2. _____

My daily push mindset:

1. _____
_____
_____
_____
_____
_____
_____

Date: ___/___/_____

Effective people are not problem-minded; they're opportunity-minded. They feed opportunities and starve problems.
—Stephen Covey

I am grateful for:

1. _____
2. _____
3. _____

My commitments today:

1. _____
2. _____

My daily push mindset:

1. _____

_____

_____

_____

_____

_____

_____

Date: ___/___/___

A professional is a person who can do his best at a time when he doesn't particularly feel like it. —Alistair Cooke

I am grateful for:

1. _____
2. _____
3. _____

My commitments today:

1. _____
2. _____

My daily push mindset:

1. _____
_____
_____
_____
_____
_____
_____

Date: ____ / ___ / _____

Whatever your grade or position, if you know how and when to speak, and when to remain silent, your chances of real success are proportionately increased. —Ralph C. Smedley

I am grateful for:

1. _____
2. _____
3. _____

My commitments today:

1. _____
2. _____

My daily push mindset:

1. _____

_____

_____

_____

_____

_____

_____

Date: ___/___/___

I do not think there is any other quality so essential to success of any kind as the quality of perseverance. It overcomes almost everything, even nature. —John D. Rockefeller

I am grateful for:

1. _____
2. _____
3. _____

My commitments today:

1. _____
2. _____

My daily push mindset:

1. _____

_____

_____

_____

_____

_____

Date: ___/___/___

I know the price of success: dedication, hard work and an unremitting devotion to the things you want to see happen.
—Frank Lloyd Wright

I am grateful for:

1. _____
2. _____
3. _____

My commitments today:

1. _____
2. _____

My daily push mindset:

1. _____

_____

_____

_____

_____

_____

_____

WEEKLY REFLECTION FOR MY DAILY PUSH JOURNAL

We also want you to commit to 100% participation in this reflection once a week.

The guidelines to give you the best success are:

1. Find a quiet place that is technology- and people-free (aside from music that may lend to focus)

2. Do not rush, stay present, enjoy the journey

3. Find takeaways from each area of evaluation (what you learned, what you need to improve on, what is working, etc.)

Everyone has a way to give this amount of time to their success every week.

Topic to reflect on:

1. *Practice, Practice, Practice*

   a. What areas in the last week have you shown discipline, outlined a routine, or demonstrated strong time management?

   _____

   _____

   b. What areas in the last week need improvement or more practice in the week ahead?

   _____

   _____

   _____

2. *Just Keep Going*

    a. In the last week, how have you demonstrated perseverance or resilience?

    b. What can you do in the week ahead to improve and/or help others improve in their perseverance or resilience?

3. *Rise Up*

    a. This week, how have you shown confidence, courage, and/or humility?

    b. What can you do in the week ahead to work on and improve in these areas?

4. *Keeping Score*

    a. This week, what have you done to hold yourself or others accountable?

b. What are some areas in the week ahead where you can do a better job of keeping score?

_____

_____

_____

c. Have you checked in with your accountability partner(s) lately?

_____

_____

_____

5. *Huddle*

a. This week, what have you done to build your team or improve teamwork personally and/ or professionally?

_____

_____

_____

b. How can you improve on or strengthen the teams you are a part of, this coming week?

_____

_____

_____

6. *Fierce*

a. Over the past week when have you demonstrated assertiveness, aggressiveness, or competitiveness?

_____

_____

_____

b. Next week, what can you do to use these qualities to your advantage?

7. *Triumph*

a. How have you demonstrated leadership qualities this week?

b. What can you do to improve or enhance your leadership skills in the coming week and better execute your game plan?

Using concepts that you learned from reading each principle, evaluate where you are at with these areas. Incorporate visualizations to support what you want to see yourself doing and how it feels to have accomplished them.

You are deserving of your triumph! Now it's time to start working to create it.

Take a few deep breaths, visualize and see this in the present moment completed.

Date: ___ / ___ / ___

Do not fear to be eccentric in opinion, for every opinion now accepted was once eccentric. —Bertrand Russell

I am grateful for:

1. _____
2. _____
3. _____

My commitments today:

1. _____
2. _____

My daily push mindset:

1. _____

_____

_____

_____

_____

_____

Date: / /

Each problem has hidden in it an opportunity so powerful that it literally dwarfs the problem. The greatest success stories were created by people who recognized a problem and turned it into an opportunity. —Joseph Sugarman

I am grateful for:

1. _____
2. _____
3. _____

My commitments today:

1. _____
2. _____

My daily push mindset:

1. _____

_____

_____

_____

_____

_____

_____

Date: ___/___/_____

Fortunate is the person who has developed the self-control to steer a straight course towards his objective in life, without being swayed from his purpose by either commendation or condemnation. —Napoleon Hill

I am grateful for:

1. _____
2. _____
3. _____

My commitments today:

1. _____
2. _____

My daily push mindset:

1. _____

_____

_____

_____

_____

_____

_____

Date: ___/___/___

Never let your work drive you. Master it and keep it in complete control. —Booker T. Washington

I am grateful for:

1. _____
2. _____
3. _____

My commitments today:

1. _____
2. _____

My daily push mindset:

1. _____

_____

_____

_____

_____

_____

_____

Date: / /

Follow your dream as long as you live, do not lessen the time of
following desire, for wasting time is an abomination of the spirit.
—Plato

I am grateful for:

1.
2.
3.

My commitments today:

1.
2.

My daily push mindset:

1.

Date: ___ / ___ / ___

You say I started out with practically nothing, but that isn't correct. We all start with all there is. It's how we use it that makes things possible. —Henry Ford

I am grateful for:

1. _____
2. _____
3. _____

My commitments today:

1. _____
2. _____

My daily push mindset:

1. _____

_____

_____

_____

_____

_____

_____

Weekly Reflection for My Daily Push Journal

We also want you to commit to 100% participation in this reflection once a week.

The guidelines to give you the best success are:

1. Find a quiet place that is technology- and people-free (aside from music that may lend to focus)

2. Do not rush, stay present, enjoy the journey

3. Find takeaways from each area of evaluation (what you learned, what you need to improve on, what is working, etc.)

Everyone has a way to give this amount of time to their success every week.

Topic to reflect on:

1. *Practice, Practice, Practice*

   a. What areas in the last week have you shown discipline, outlined a routine, or demonstrated strong time management?

   _____

   _____

   _____

   b. What areas in the last week need improvement or more practice in the week ahead?

   _____

   _____

   _____

2. *Just Keep Going*

    a. In the last week, how have you demonstrated perseverance or resilience?

_____

_____

_____

    b. What can you do in the week ahead to improve and/or help others improve in their perseverance or resilience?

_____

_____

_____

3. *Rise Up*

    a. This week, how have you shown confidence, courage, and/or humility?

_____

_____

_____

    b. What can you do in the week ahead to work on and improve in these areas?

_____

_____

_____

4. *Keeping Score*

    a. This week, what have you done to hold yourself or others accountable?

_____

_____

_____

b. What are some areas in the week ahead where you can do a better job of keeping score?

_____

_____

_____

c. Have you checked in with your accountability partner(s) lately?

_____

_____

_____

5. *Huddle*

   a. This week, what have you done to build your team or improve teamwork personally and/ or professionally?

_____

_____

_____

   b. How can you improve on or strengthen the teams you are a part of, this coming week?

_____

_____

_____

6. *Fierce*

   a. Over the past week when have you demonstrated assertiveness, aggressiveness, or competitiveness?

_____

_____

_____

b. Next week, what can you do to use these qualities to your advantage?

7. *Triumph*

a. How have you demonstrated leadership qualities this week?

b. What can you do to improve or enhance your leadership skills in the coming week and better execute your game plan?

Using concepts that you learned from reading each principle, evaluate where you are at with these areas. Incorporate visualizations to support what you want to see yourself doing and how it feels to have accomplished them.

You are deserving of your triumph! Now it's time to start working to create it.

Take a few deep breaths, visualize and see this in the present moment completed.

Date: ___/___/_____

I don't have to be what nobody else wants me to be and I am not afraid to be what I want to be. —Muhammad Ali

I am grateful for:

1. _____
2. _____
3. _____

My commitments today:

1. _____
2. _____

My daily push mindset:

1. _____

_____

_____

_____

_____

_____

_____

Date: ___/___/_____

The highest reward for one's toil is not what one gets for it, but what one becomes by it. —John Ruskin

I am grateful for:

1. _____
2. _____
3. _____

My commitments today:

1. _____
2. _____

My daily push mindset:

1. _____

_____

_____

_____

_____

_____

_____

Date: ___/___/_____

The seat of freedom is reserved for the man who lives by his own work, and in that work, does what he wants to do.
—George Robin Collingwood

I am grateful for:

1. _____
2. _____
3. _____

My commitments today:

1. _____
2. _____

My daily push mindset:

1. _____

_____

_____

_____

_____

_____

_____

Date: ___/___/_____

> *The difference between success and mediocrity is all in the way you think.* —Dean Francis

I am grateful for:

1. _____
2. _____
3. _____

My commitments today:

1. _____
2. _____

My daily push mindset:

1. _____
_____
_____
_____
_____
_____
_____

Date: ___/___/___

You are never too old to set another goal or to dream a new dream. —Les Brown

I am grateful for:

1. _____
2. _____
3. _____

My commitments today:

1. _____
2. _____

My daily push mindset:

1. _____

_____

_____

_____

_____

_____

_____

Date: ___/___/_____

What separates those who achieve from those who do not is in direct proportion to one's ability to ask for help.

—Donald Keough

I am grateful for:

1. _____
2. _____
3. _____

My commitments today:

1. _____
2. _____

My daily push mindset:

1. _____

_____

_____

_____

_____

_____

_____

Weekly Reflection for My Daily Push Journal

We also want you to commit to 100% participation in this reflection once a week.

The guidelines to give you the best success are:

1. Find a quiet place that is technology- and people-free (aside from music that may lend to focus)

2. Do not rush, stay present, enjoy the journey

3. Find takeaways from each area of evaluation (what you learned, what you need to improve on, what is working, etc.)

Everyone has a way to give this amount of time to their success every week.

Topic to reflect on:

1. *Practice, Practice, Practice*

   a. What areas in the last week have you shown discipline, outlined a routine, or demonstrated strong time management?

   _____

   _____

   b. What areas in the last week need improvement or more practice in the week ahead?

   _____

   _____

   _____

2. *Just Keep Going*

   a. In the last week, how have you demonstrated perseverance or resilience?

   b. What can you do in the week ahead to improve and/or help others improve in their perseverance or resilience?

3. *Rise Up*

   a. This week, how have you shown confidence, courage, and/or humility?

   b. What can you do in the week ahead to work on and improve in these areas?

4. *Keeping Score*

   a. This week, what have you done to hold yourself or others accountable?

b. What are some areas in the week ahead where you can do a better job of keeping score?

c. Have you checked in with your accountability partner(s) lately?

5. *Huddle*

a. This week, what have you done to build your team or improve teamwork personally and/ or professionally?

b. How can you improve on or strengthen the teams you are a part of, this coming week?

6. *Fierce*

a. Over the past week when have you demonstrated assertiveness, aggressiveness, or competitiveness?

b. Next week, what can you do to use these qualities to your advantage?

_____

_____

_____

_____

7. *Triumph*

   a. How have you demonstrated leadership qualities this week?

_____

_____

_____

_____

   b. What can you do to improve or enhance your leadership skills in the coming week and better execute your game plan?

_____

_____

_____

_____

Using concepts that you learned from reading each principle, evaluate where you are at with these areas. Incorporate visualizations to support what you want to see yourself doing and how it feels to have accomplished them.

You are deserving of your triumph! Now it's time to start working to create it.

Take a few deep breaths, visualize and see this in the present moment completed.

Date: ___/___/___

You only have to do a very few things right in your life so long as you don't do too many things wrong. —Warren Buffett

I am grateful for:

1. _____
2. _____
3. _____

My commitments today:

1. _____
2. _____

My daily push mindset:

1. _____

_____

_____

_____

_____

_____

Date: ___/___/_____

It is wise to keep in mind that neither success nor failure is ever final. —Roger Babson

I am grateful for:

1. _____
2. _____
3. _____

My commitments today:

1. _____
2. _____

My daily push mindset:

1. _____

_____

_____

_____

_____

_____

_____

Date: ___/___/_____

Success is a journey, not a destination. —Ben Sweetland

I am grateful for:

1. _____
2. _____
3. _____

My commitments today:

1. _____
2. _____

My daily push mindset:

1. _____

_____

_____

_____

_____

_____

_____

Date: ___/___/_____

To guarantee success, act as if it were impossible to fail.
—Dorothea Brande

I am grateful for:

1. _____
2. _____
3. _____

My commitments today:

1. _____
2. _____

My daily push mindset:

1. _____

_____

_____

_____

_____

_____

_____

Date: ___/___/_____

Success is often the result of taking a misstep in the right direction.
—Al Bernstein

I am grateful for:

1. _____
2. _____
3. _____

My commitments today:

1. _____
2. _____

My daily push mindset:

1. _____

_____

_____

_____

_____

_____

_____

Date: ___/___/_____

You can do it if you believe you can. —Napoleon Hill

I am grateful for:

1. _____
2. _____
3. _____

My commitments today:

1. _____
2. _____

My daily push mindset:

1. _____
_____
_____
_____
_____
_____
_____

WEEKLY REFLECTION FOR MY DAILY PUSH JOURNAL

We also want you to commit to 100% participation in this reflection once a week.

The guidelines to give you the best success are:

1. Find a quiet place that is technology- and people-free (aside from music that may lend to focus)

2. Do not rush, stay present, enjoy the journey

3. Find takeaways from each area of evaluation (what you learned, what you need to improve on, what is working, etc.)

Everyone has a way to give this amount of time to their success every week.

Topic to reflect on:

1. *Practice, Practice, Practice*

   a. What areas in the last week have you shown discipline, outlined a routine, or demonstrated strong time management?

   _____

   _____

   _____

   b. What areas in the last week need improvement or more practice in the week ahead?

   _____

   _____

   _____

2. *Just Keep Going*

   a. In the last week, how have you demonstrated perseverance or resilience?

....

....

....

   b. What can you do in the week ahead to improve and/or help others improve in their perseverance or resilience?

....

....

....

3. *Rise Up*

   a. This week, how have you shown confidence, courage, and/or humility?

....

....

....

   b. What can you do in the week ahead to work on and improve in these areas?

....

....

....

4. *Keeping Score*

   a. This week, what have you done to hold yourself or others accountable?

....

....

....

b. What are some areas in the week ahead where you can do a better job of keeping score?

_____

_____

_____

c. Have you checked in with your accountability partner(s) lately?

_____

_____

_____

5. *Huddle*

a. This week, what have you done to build your team or improve teamwork personally and/ or professionally?

_____

_____

_____

b. How can you improve on or strengthen the teams you are a part of, this coming week?

_____

_____

_____

6. *Fierce*

a. Over the past week when have you demonstrated assertiveness, aggressiveness, or competitiveness?

_____

_____

_____

b. Next week, what can you do to use these qualities to your advantage?

_____

_____

_____

_____

7. *Triumph*

   a. How have you demonstrated leadership qualities this week?

_____

_____

_____

_____

   b. What can you do to improve or enhance your leadership skills in the coming week and better execute your game plan?

_____

_____

_____

_____

Using concepts that you learned from reading each principle, evaluate where you are at with these areas. Incorporate visualizations to support what you want to see yourself doing and how it feels to have accomplished them.

You are deserving of your triumph! Now it's time to start working to create it.

Take a few deep breaths, visualize and see this in the present moment completed.

Date: ___ / ___ / _____

Success is simply a matter of luck. Ask any failure.

—Earl Wilson

I am grateful for:

1. _____
2. _____
3. _____

My commitments today:

1. _____
2. _____

My daily push mindset:

1. _____

_____

_____

_____

_____

_____

_____

Date: ___/___/_____

I like a state of continual becoming, with a goal in front and not behind. —George Bernard Shaw

I am grateful for:

1. _____
2. _____
3. _____

My commitments today:

1. _____
2. _____

My daily push mindset:

1. _____

_____

_____

_____

_____

_____

_____

Date: ___ / ___ / ___

You must do the very thing you think you cannot do.
—Eleanor Roosevelt

I am grateful for:

1. _____
2. _____
3. _____

My commitments today:

1. _____
2. _____

My daily push mindset:

1. _____

_____

_____

_____

_____

_____

_____

Date: ___/___/___

Flaming enthusiasm, backed by horse-sense and persistence, is the quality that most frequently makes for success.

—Dale Carnegie

I am grateful for:

1. _____
2. _____
3. _____

My commitments today:

1. _____
2. _____

My daily push mindset:

1. _____

_____

_____

_____

_____

_____

Date: ___/___/_____

It's the repetition of affirmations that leads to belief. And once that belief becomes a deep conviction, things begin to happen.
—Claude M. Bristol

I am grateful for:

1. _____
2. _____
3. _____

My commitments today:

1. _____
2. _____

My daily push mindset:

1. _____

_____

_____

_____

_____

_____

Date: ___/___/___

The biggest temptation is to settle for too little.

—Thomas Merton

I am grateful for:

1. _____
2. _____
3. _____

My commitments today:

1. _____
2. _____

My daily push mindset:

1. _____

_____

_____

_____

_____

_____

_____

Weekly Reflection for My Daily Push Journal

We also want you to commit to 100% participation in this reflection once a week.

The guidelines to give you the best success are:

1. Find a quiet place that is technology- and people-free (aside from music that may lend to focus)

2. Do not rush, stay present, enjoy the journey

3. Find takeaways from each area of evaluation (what you learned, what you need to improve on, what is working, etc.)

Everyone has a way to give this amount of time to their success every week.

Topic to reflect on:

1. *Practice, Practice, Practice*

   a. What areas in the last week have you shown discipline, outlined a routine, or demonstrated strong time management?

   b. What areas in the last week need improvement or more practice in the week ahead?

2. *Just Keep Going*

   a. In the last week, how have you demonstrated perseverance or resilience?

   b. What can you do in the week ahead to improve and/or help others improve in their perseverance or resilience?

3. *Rise Up*

   a. This week, how have you shown confidence, courage, and/or humility?

   b. What can you do in the week ahead to work on and improve in these areas?

4. *Keeping Score*

   a. This week, what have you done to hold yourself or others accountable?

b. What are some areas in the week ahead where you can do a better job of keeping score?

_____

_____

_____

c. Have you checked in with your accountability partner(s) lately?

_____

_____

_____

5. *Huddle*

a. This week, what have you done to build your team or improve teamwork personally and/ or professionally?

_____

_____

_____

b. How can you improve on or strengthen the teams you are a part of, this coming week?

_____

_____

_____

6. *Fierce*

a. Over the past week when have you demonstrated assertiveness, aggressiveness, or competitiveness?

_____

_____

_____

b. Next week, what can you do to use these qualities to your advantage?

---

7. *Triumph*

a. How have you demonstrated leadership qualities this week?

---

b. What can you do to improve or enhance your leadership skills in the coming week and better execute your game plan?

Using concepts that you learned from reading each principle, evaluate where you are at with these areas. Incorporate visualizations to support what you want to see yourself doing and how it feels to have accomplished them.

You are deserving of your triumph! Now it's time to start working to create it.

Take a few deep breaths, visualize and see this in the present moment completed.

Date: ___/___/___

Yes, I am a dreamer. For a dreamer is one who can find his way by moonlight, and see the dawn before the rest of the world.
—Oscar Wilde

I am grateful for:

1. _____
2. _____
3. _____

My commitments today:

1. _____
2. _____

My daily push mindset:

1. _____
_____
_____
_____
_____
_____
_____

Date: ___/___/_____

Don't dream it. Be it! —Richard O'Brian

I am grateful for:

1. _____
2. _____
3. _____

My commitments today:

1. _____
2. _____

My daily push mindset:

1. _____

_____

_____

_____

_____

_____

_____

Date: ___/___/_____

He has achieved success who has lived well, laughed often and loved much. —Bessie Anderson Stanley

I am grateful for:

1. _____
2. _____
3. _____

My commitments today:

1. _____
2. _____

My daily push mindset:

1. _____

_____

_____

_____

_____

_____

_____

Date: ___/___/_____

*If you don't go after what you want, you'll never have it. If you
don't ask, the answer is always no. If you don't step forward,
you're always in the same place.* —Nora Roberts

I am grateful for:

1. _____
2. _____
3. _____

My commitments today:

1. _____
2. _____

My daily push mindset:

1. _____

_____

_____

_____

_____

_____

_____

Date: / /

Henry Ford could get anything out of men because he just talked and would tell them stories. He'd never say, 'I want this done!' He'd say, 'I wonder if we can do it.' —George Brown

I am grateful for:

1. _____
2. _____
3. _____

My commitments today:

1. _____
2. _____

My daily push mindset:

1. _____

_____

_____

_____

_____

_____

Date: ___ / ___ / ___

Those who dream by day are cognizant of many things which escape those who dream only by night. —Edgar Allen Poe

I am grateful for:

1. _____
2. _____
3. _____

My commitments today:

1. _____
2. _____

My daily push mindset:

1. _____

_____

_____

_____

_____

_____

_____

Weekly Reflection for My Daily Push Journal

We also want you to commit to 100% participation in this reflection once a week.

The guidelines to give you the best success are:

1. Find a quiet place that is technology- and people-free (aside from music that may lend to focus)

2. Do not rush, stay present, enjoy the journey

3. Find takeaways from each area of evaluation (what you learned, what you need to improve on, what is working, etc.)

Everyone has a way to give this amount of time to their success every week.

Topic to reflect on:

1. *Practice, Practice, Practice*

   a. What areas in the last week have you shown discipline, outlined a routine, or demonstrated strong time management?

   b. What areas in the last week need improvement or more practice in the week ahead?

2. *Just Keep Going*

   a. In the last week, how have you demonstrated perseverance or resilience?

   b. What can you do in the week ahead to improve and/or help others improve in their perseverance or resilience?

3. *Rise Up*

   a. This week, how have you shown confidence, courage, and/or humility?

   b. What can you do in the week ahead to work on and improve in these areas?

4. *Keeping Score*

   a. This week, what have you done to hold yourself or others accountable?

b. What are some areas in the week ahead where you can do a better job of keeping score?

_____

_____

_____

c. Have you checked in with your accountability partner(s) lately?

_____

_____

_____

5. *Huddle*

a. This week, what have you done to build your team or improve teamwork personally and/ or professionally?

_____

_____

_____

b. How can you improve on or strengthen the teams you are a part of, this coming week?

_____

_____

_____

6. *Fierce*

a. Over the past week when have you demonstrated assertiveness, aggressiveness, or competitiveness?

_____

_____

_____

b. Next week, what can you do to use these qualities to your advantage?

_____

_____

_____

_____

7. *Triumph*

a. How have you demonstrated leadership qualities this week?

_____

_____

_____

_____

b. What can you do to improve or enhance your leadership skills in the coming week and better execute your game plan?

_____

_____

_____

_____

Using concepts that you learned from reading each principle, evaluate where you are at with these areas. Incorporate visualizations to support what you want to see yourself doing and how it feels to have accomplished them.

You are deserving of your triumph! Now it's time to start working to create it.

Take a few deep breaths, visualize and see this in the present moment completed.

Date: ___ / ___ / ___

The key to happiness is having dreams; the key to success is making them come true. —James Allen

I am grateful for:

1. _____

2. _____

3. _____

My commitments today:

1. _____

2. _____

My daily push mindset:

1. _____

_____

_____

_____

_____

_____

Date: ___/___/_____

Life is a series of problem-solving opportunities. The problems you face will either defeat you or develop you depending on how you respond to them. —Rick Warren

I am grateful for:

1. _____
2. _____
3. _____

My commitments today:

1. _____
2. _____

My daily push mindset:

1. _____

_____

_____

_____

_____

_____

_____

Date: ___/___/___

All men who have achieved great things have been great dreamers. —Orison Swett Marden

I am grateful for:

1. _____
2. _____
3. _____

My commitments today:

1. _____
2. _____

My daily push mindset:

1. _____

_____

_____

_____

_____

_____

_____

Date: ___/___/_____

Success is doing ordinary things extraordinarily well.

—Jim Rohn

I am grateful for:

1. _____
2. _____
3. _____

My commitments today:

1. _____
2. _____

My daily push mindset:

1. _____

_____

_____

_____

_____

_____

_____

Date: ___ / ___ / ___

I start with the premise that the function of leadership is to produce more leaders, not more followers. —Ralph Nader

I am grateful for:

1. _____
2. _____
3. _____

My commitments today:

1. _____
2. _____

My daily push mindset:

1. _____

_____

_____

_____

_____

_____

_____

Date: ___/___/_____

> *Never walk away from failure. On the contrary, study it*
> *carefully and imaginatively for its hidden assets.*
> —Michael Korda

I am grateful for:

1. _____
2. _____
3. _____

My commitments today:

1. _____
2. _____

My daily push mindset:

1. _____

_____

_____

_____

_____

_____

_____

WEEKLY REFLECTION FOR MY DAILY PUSH JOURNAL

We also want you to commit to 100% participation in this reflection once a week.

The guidelines to give you the best success are:

1. Find a quiet place that is technology- and people-free (aside from music that may lend to focus)

2. Do not rush, stay present, enjoy the journey

3. Find takeaways from each area of evaluation (what you learned, what you need to improve on, what is working, etc.)

Everyone has a way to give this amount of time to their success every week.

Topic to reflect on:

1. *Practice, Practice, Practice*

   a. What areas in the last week have you shown discipline, outlined a routine, or demonstrated strong time management?

   b. What areas in the last week need improvement or more practice in the week ahead?

2. *Just Keep Going*

   a. In the last week, how have you demonstrated perseverance or resilience?

   b. What can you do in the week ahead to improve and/or help others improve in their perseverance or resilience?

3. *Rise Up*

   a. This week, how have you shown confidence, courage, and/or humility?

   b. What can you do in the week ahead to work on and improve in these areas?

4. *Keeping Score*

   a. This week, what have you done to hold yourself or others accountable?

b. What are some areas in the week ahead where you can do a better job of keeping score?

c. Have you checked in with your accountability partner(s) lately?

5. *Huddle*

   a. This week, what have you done to build your team or improve teamwork personally and/ or professionally?

   b. How can you improve on or strengthen the teams you are a part of, this coming week?

6. *Fierce*

   a. Over the past week when have you demonstrated assertiveness, aggressiveness, or competitiveness?

b. Next week, what can you do to use these qualities to your advantage?

_____

_____

_____

_____

7. *Triumph*

a. How have you demonstrated leadership qualities this week?

_____

_____

_____

b. What can you do to improve or enhance your leadership skills in the coming week and better execute your game plan?

_____

_____

_____

Using concepts that you learned from reading each principle, evaluate where you are at with these areas. Incorporate visualizations to support what you want to see yourself doing and how it feels to have accomplished them.

You are deserving of your triumph! Now it's time to start working to create it.

Take a few deep breaths, visualize and see this in the present moment completed.

Date: _____ / ___ / _____

Nothing ever comes to one that is worth having except as a result of hard work. —Booker T. Washington

I am grateful for:

1. _____

2. _____

3. _____

My commitments today:

1. _____

2. _____

My daily push mindset:

1. _____

_____

_____

_____

_____

_____

Date: ___/___/_____

If you have the will to win, you have achieved half your success; if you don't, you have achieved half your failure.
—David Ambrose

I am grateful for:

1. _____
2. _____
3. _____

My commitments today:

1. _____
2. _____

My daily push mindset:

1. _____

_____

_____

_____

_____

_____

_____

Date: /   /

You may be disappointed if you fail, but you are doomed if you don't try. —Beverly Sills

I am grateful for:

1. _____
2. _____
3. _____

My commitments today:

1. _____
2. _____

My daily push mindset:

1. _____

_____

_____

_____

_____

_____

Date: ___/___/___

Unless you try to do something beyond what you have already mastered, you will never grow. —Ronald E. Osborn

I am grateful for:

1. _____
2. _____
3. _____

My commitments today:

1. _____
2. _____

My daily push mindset:

1. _____

_____

_____

_____

_____

_____

_____

Date: ___/___/_____

Successful and unsuccessful people do not vary greatly in their abilities. They vary in their desires to reach their potential.

—John Maxwell

I am grateful for:

1. _____

2. _____

3. _____

My commitments today:

1. _____

2. _____

My daily push mindset:

1. _____

_____

_____

_____

_____

_____

_____

Date: ___/___/___

The only difference between a success and a failure is that the successful person is willing to do what the failure is not willing to do.
—J.R. Ridinger

I am grateful for:

1. _____
2. _____
3. _____

My commitments today:

1. _____
2. _____

My daily push mindset:

1. _____

_____

_____

_____

_____

_____

_____

Weekly Reflection for My Daily Push Journal

We also want you to commit to 100% participation in this reflection once a week.

The guidelines to give you the best success are:

1. Find a quiet place that is technology- and people-free (aside from music that may lend to focus)

2. Do not rush, stay present, enjoy the journey

3. Find takeaways from each area of evaluation (what you learned, what you need to improve on, what is working, etc.)

Everyone has a way to give this amount of time to their success every week.

Topic to reflect on:

1. *Practice, Practice, Practice*

   a. What areas in the last week have you shown discipline, outlined a routine, or demonstrated strong time management?

   _____

   _____

   _____

   b. What areas in the last week need improvement or more practice in the week ahead?

   _____

   _____

   _____

2. *Just Keep Going*

   a. In the last week, how have you demonstrated perseverance or resilience?

   b. What can you do in the week ahead to improve and/or help others improve in their perseverance or resilience?

3. *Rise Up*

   a. This week, how have you shown confidence, courage, and/or humility?

   b. What can you do in the week ahead to work on and improve in these areas?

4. *Keeping Score*

   a. This week, what have you done to hold yourself or others accountable?

b. What are some areas in the week ahead where you can do a better job of keeping score?

c. Have you checked in with your accountability partner(s) lately?

5. *Huddle*

a. This week, what have you done to build your team or improve teamwork personally and/ or professionally?

b. How can you improve on or strengthen the teams you are a part of, this coming week?

6. *Fierce*

a. Over the past week when have you demonstrated assertiveness, aggressiveness, or competitiveness?

b. Next week, what can you do to use these qualities to your advantage?

---

7. *Triumph*

    a. How have you demonstrated leadership qualities this week?

---

    b. What can you do to improve or enhance your leadership skills in the coming week and better execute your game plan?

Using concepts that you learned from reading each principle, evaluate where you are at with these areas. Incorporate visualizations to support what you want to see yourself doing and how it feels to have accomplished them.

You are deserving of your triumph! Now it's time to start working to create it.

Take a few deep breaths, visualize and see this in the present moment completed.

www.ingramcontent.com/pod-product-compliance
Lightning Source LLC
Chambersburg PA
CBHW072003090426
42740CB00011B/2064